Stitched with Love for

Specially Sewn

For: _____

By: _____

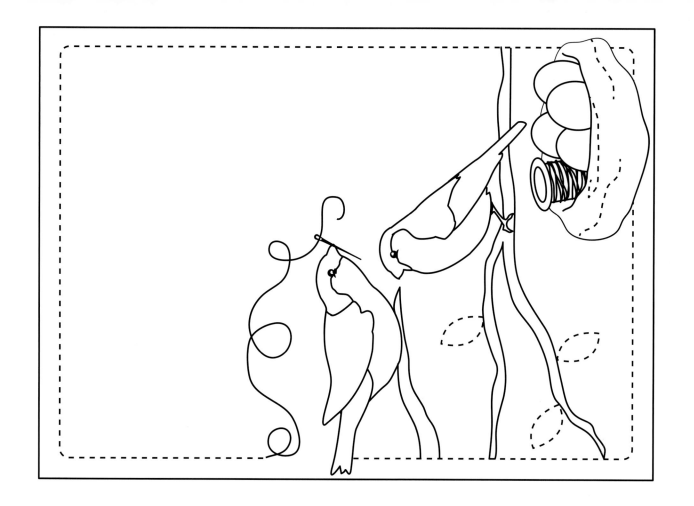

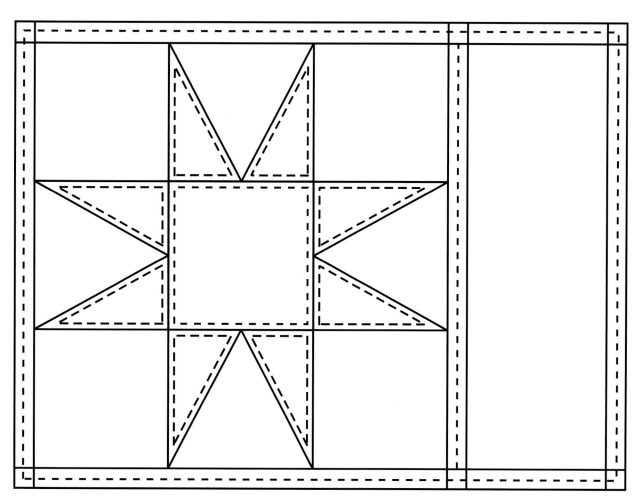

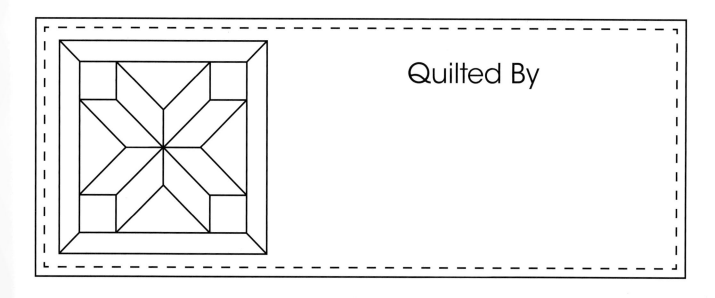

Quilted By

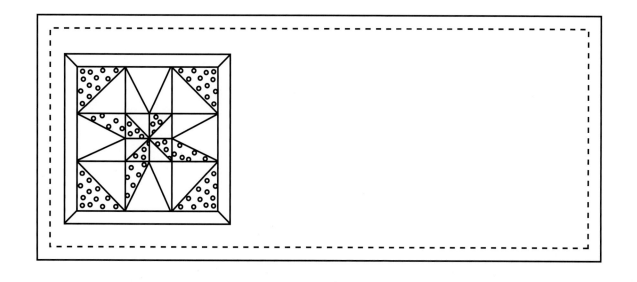

Stitched With Love:

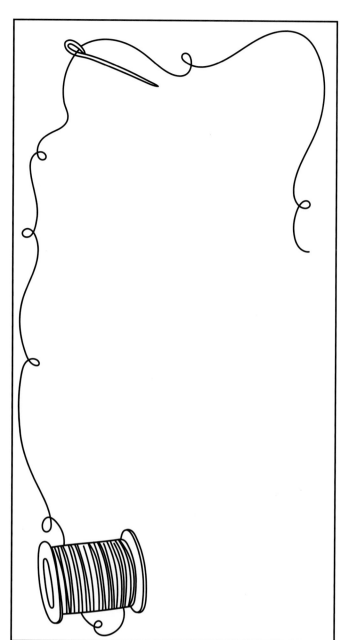

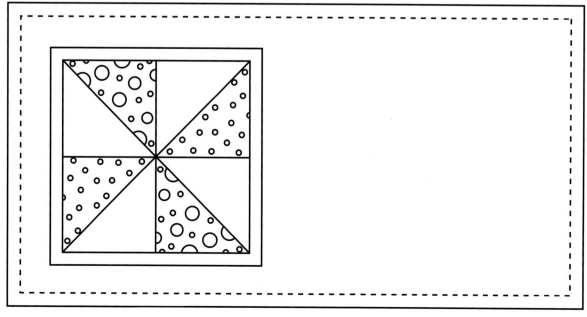

Use for Tracing

Made with
Tender Loving Care

For You

Quilted for:

By:

Date:

For: _____

By: _____

Date: _____

A Gift for You

Use for Tracing

For You!

For You

Use for Tracing

Made for:

By:

Especially for:

By:

Date:

Use for Tracing

For You

Use for Tracing

On Your Wedding Day

Welcome, Little One!

Handmade for:

_____

By:

_____

Date:

_____

welcome baby

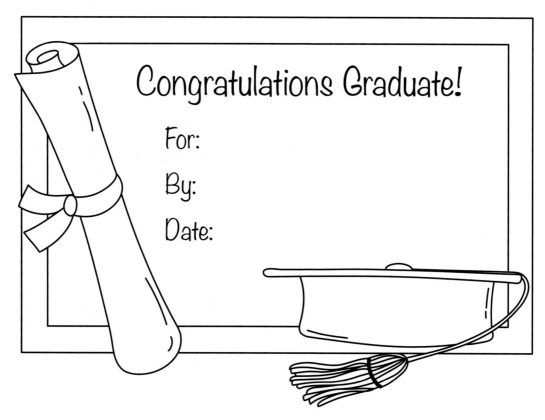

Congratulations Graduate!

For:

By:

Date:

A Mother's Love is the Heart of a Family

Happy Anniversary

Blessings on Your First Communion

Use for Tracing

sweet baby boy

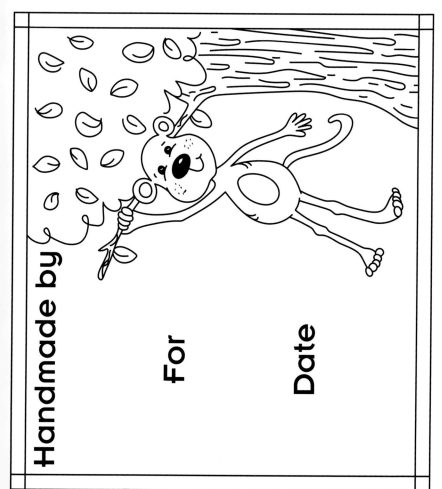

Handmade by

For

Date

precious baby girl

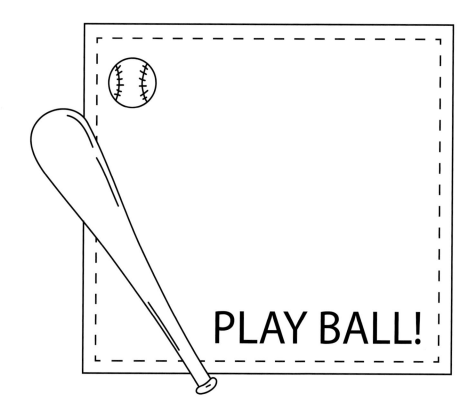

PLAY BALL!

For:

By:

Date:

To:

From:

Stitched for:

By:

Use for Tracing

Once Upon a Time...

To: _____

Stitched by: _____

Date: _____

A Gift for You

Made by:

For:

Date:

Made With Love for:

QUILTED BY:

DATE:

Made for:

By:

Date:

Quilted for a Favorite Teacher

land of the free, home of the brave

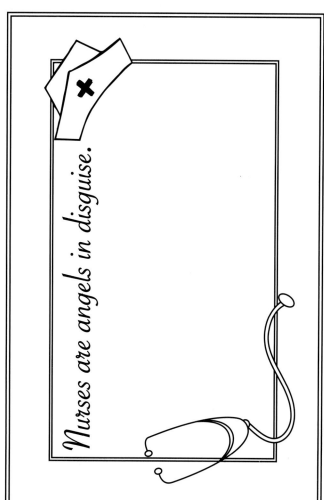

Nurses are angels in disguise.

Quilted for:

By:

Handmade by:

Faith, Hope, Love

Made With Love by:

noel

for:

from:

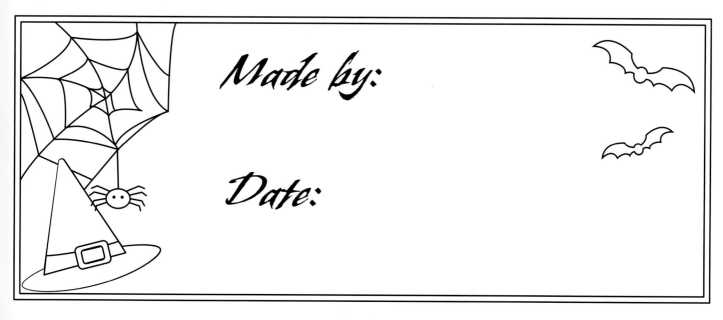

Made by:

Date:

For:

By:

Date:

Merry Christmas!

merry & bright

Made by:

For:

Date"

For Somebunny Special

Use for Tracing

Stitched with Love for

Specially Sewn

For

By

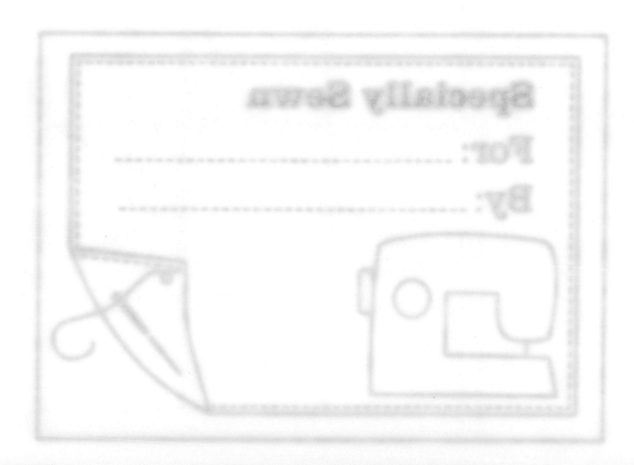

Stitched with
Love for

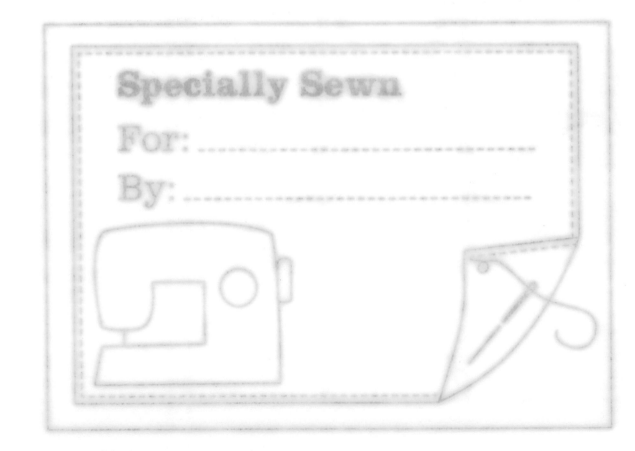

Specially Sewn

For: ------------------------------

By: ------------------------------

Test Pattern

Stitched with
Love for

Test Pattern

Use for Iron-On Transferring

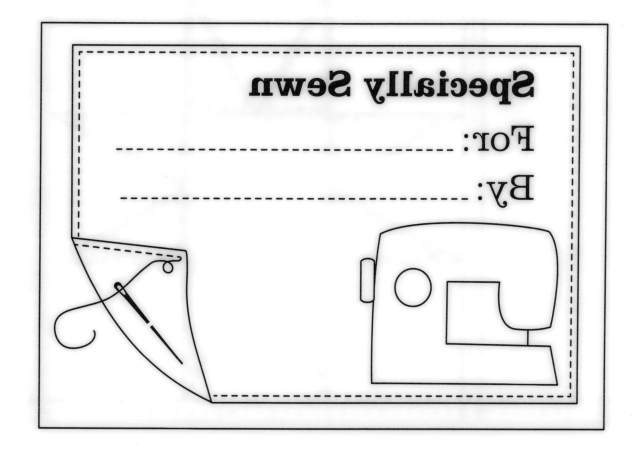

Specially Sewn

For: -----------------------

By: -----------------------

Stitched with
Love for

Test Pattern

Specially Sewn

For: -

By: -

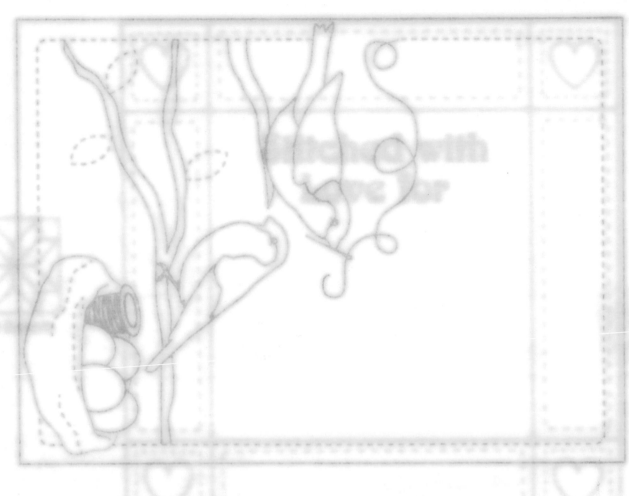

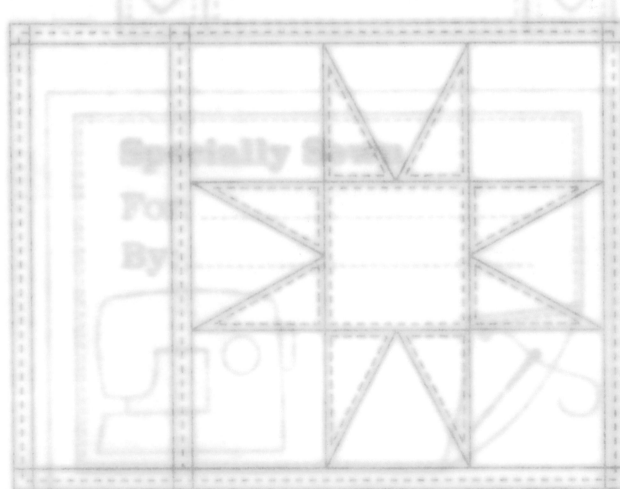

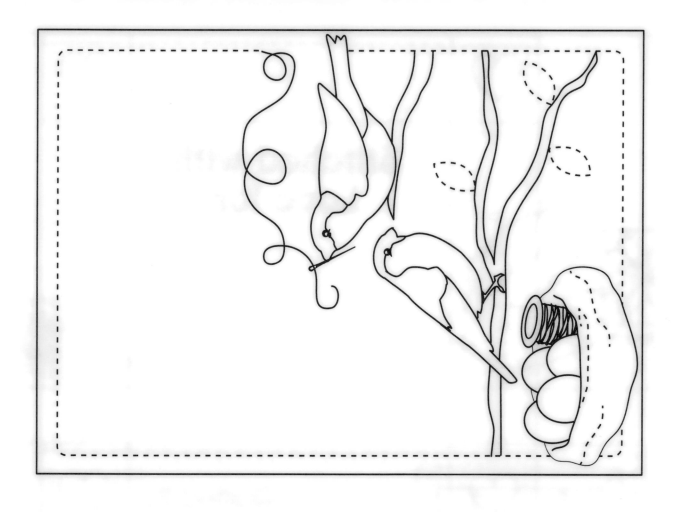

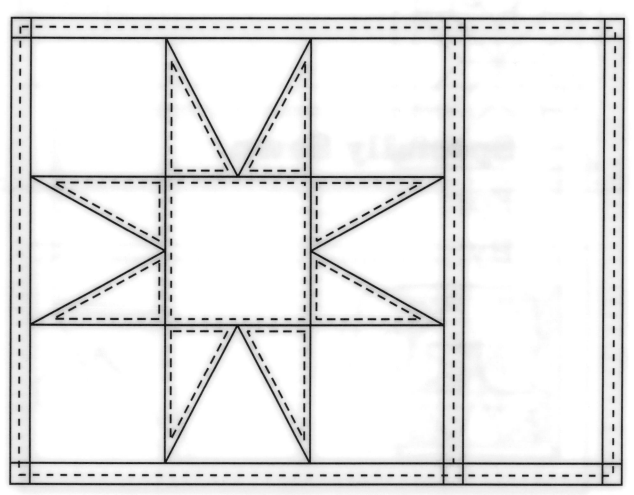

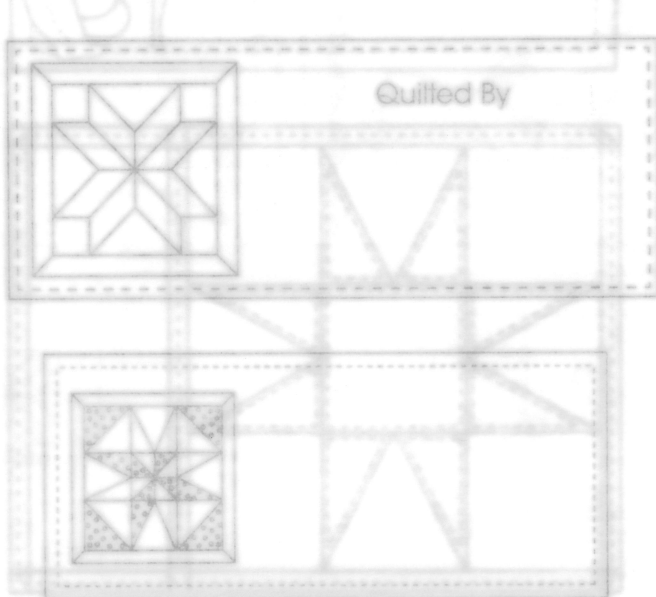

Quilted By

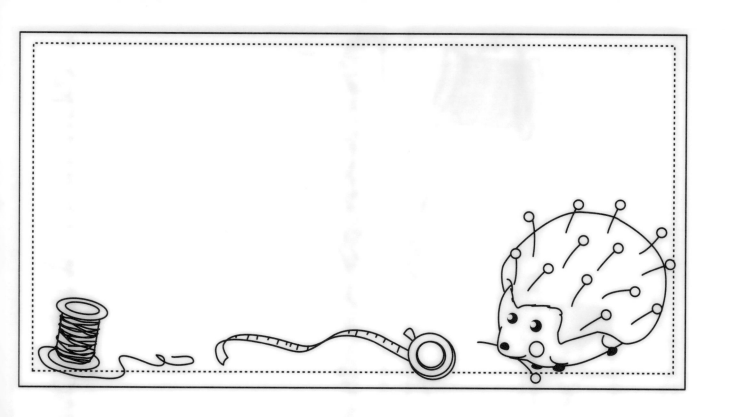

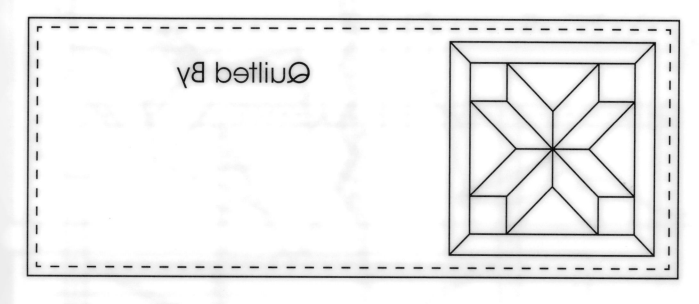

Quilted By

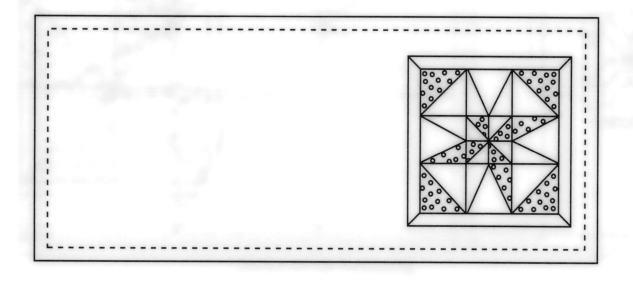

Use for Iron-On Transferring

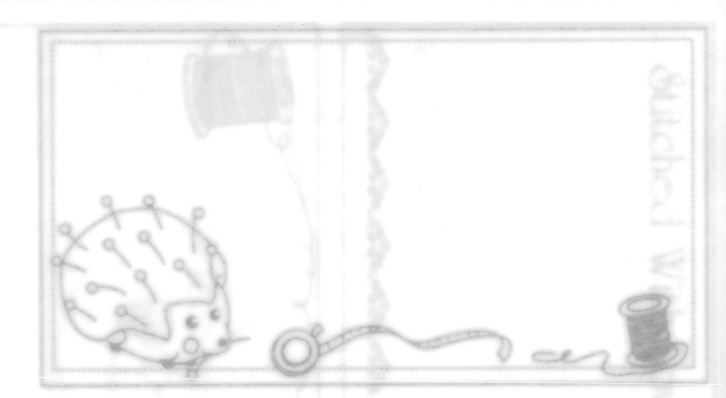

Quilted By

Stitched With Love!

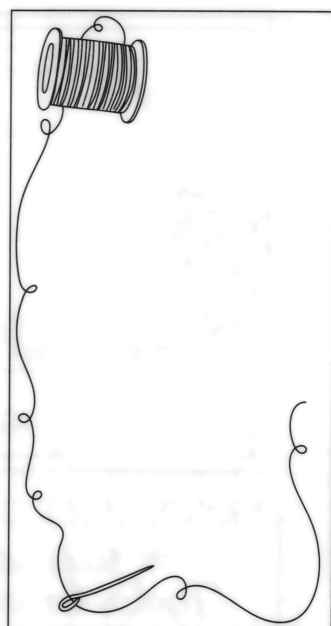

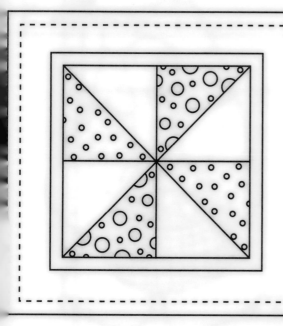

Test Pattern

Use for Iron-On Transferring

Stitched With Love.

Test Pattern

Use for Iron-On Transferring

Stitched With love.

Made with
Tender Loving Care

Stitched With Love

Made with
Tender Loving Care

Made with
Tender Loving Care

Use for Iron-On Transferring

Made with
Tender Loving Care
Quilted for

By

Date

For You

Test Pattern

Made with
Tender Loving Care

Quilted for:

By:

Date:

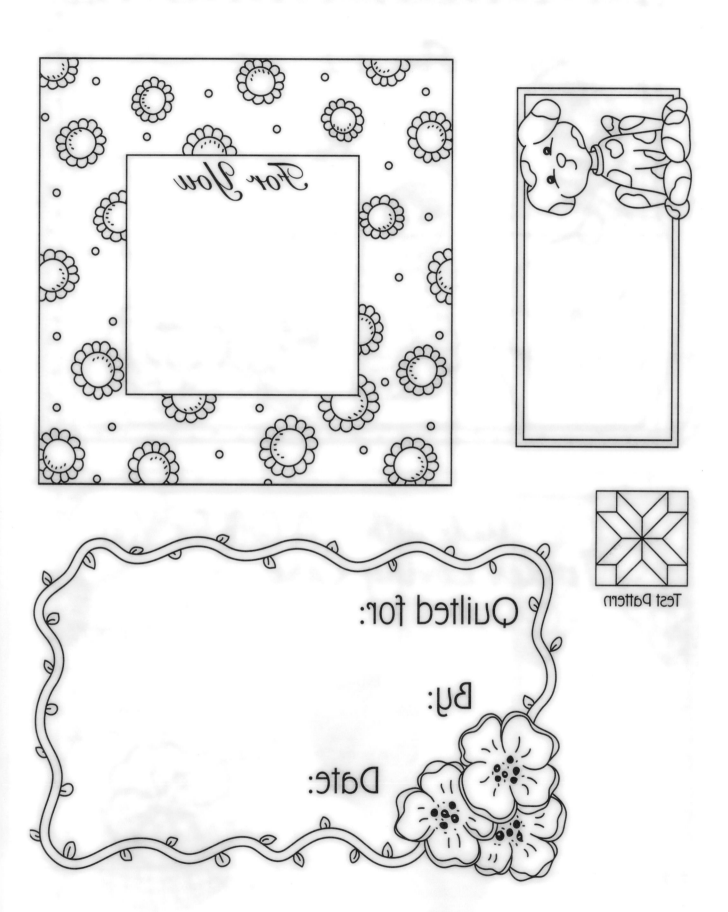

For You

Quilted for:

By:

Date:

Test Pattern

Use for Iron-On Transferring

For You

Date:

Test Pattern

Quilted for:

By:

Date:

For: _____

By: _____

Date: _____

For You

A Gift for You

For: _____

By: _____

Date: _____

A Gift for You

Use for Iron-On Transferring

For: _____

For You

By: _____

Date: _____

A Gift for You

For You!

By

Date

For You

For You!

For You

Use for Iron-On Transferring

For You!

For You

Made for:

By:

Especially for:

By:

Date:

Made for:

By:

Especially for:

By:

Date:

Use for Iron-On Transferring

Made for:

By:

Especially for:

By:

Date:

Made for:

By

For You

ecially for:

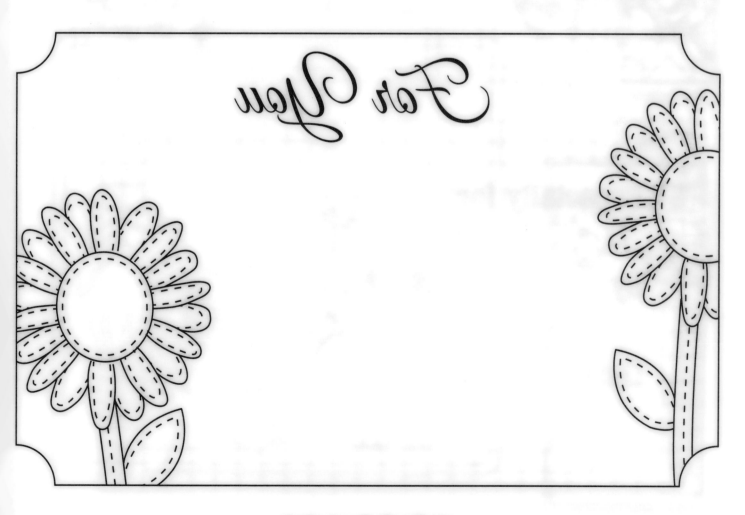

For You

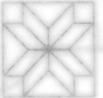

Test Pattern

For You

Test Pattern

Use for Iron-On Transferring

On Your Wedding

Test Pattern

Welcome Little One!

On Your Wedding Day

Welcome, Little One!

Handmade for:

By:

Date:

On Your Wedding Day

Welcome, Little One!

Handmade for:

By:

Date:

Test Pattern

On Your Wedding Day

Test Pattern

Welcome, Little One!

Handmade for:

By:

Date:

welcome baby

Congratulations Graduate!

For:

By:

Date:

welcome baby

Test Pattern

Test Pattern

Congratulations Graduate!

For:

By:

Date:

welcome baby

Congratulations Graduate!

For:

By:

Date:

A Mother's Love
is the Heart of a Family

Happy Anniversary

Blessings on Your First Communion

Test Pattern

Use for Iron-On Transferring

Happy Anniversary

A Mother's Love
Is the Heart of a Family

Blessings on Your First Communion

Test Pattern

sweet baby boy

BABY

A Mother's Love is the Heart of a Family

precious baby girl

Blessings on Your First Communion

Handmade by

For

Date

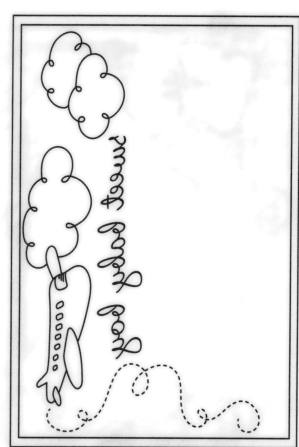

sweet baby feet

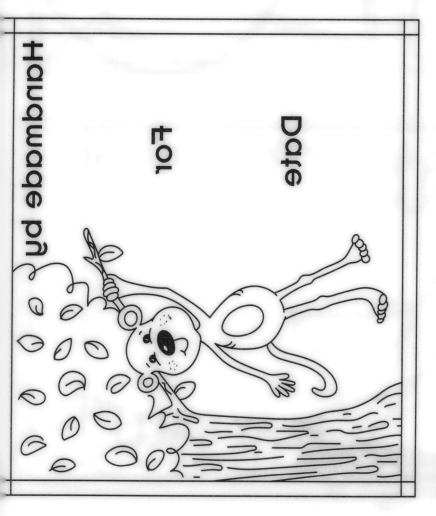

Handmade by

Date

to

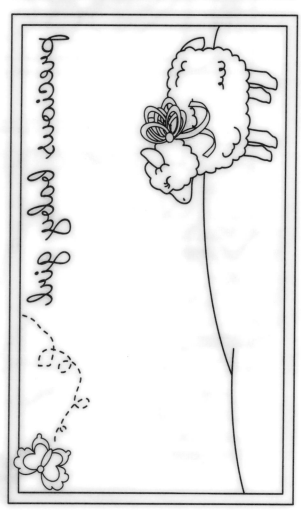

precious baby

itty bitty baby girl

Use for Iron-On Transferring

sweet baby boy

BABY

precious baby girl

Handmade by

For

Date

Test Pattern

Test Pattern

PLAY BALL!

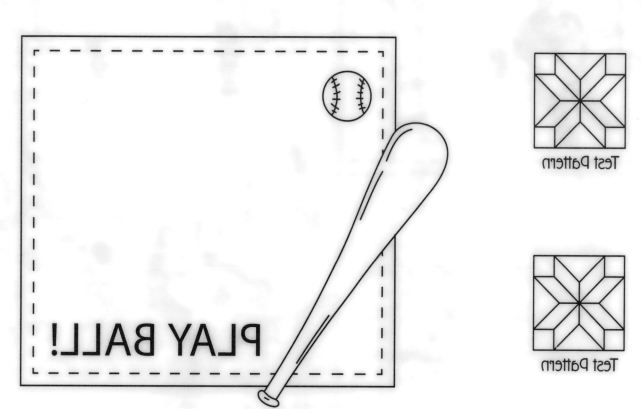

Test Pattern

Test Pattern

Use for Iron-On Transferring

To:

From:

For:

By:

Date:

Test Pattern

Test Pattern

PLAY BALL!

To:

From:

For:

By:

Date:

Stitched for:

By:

BALL!

Test Pattern

Test Pattern

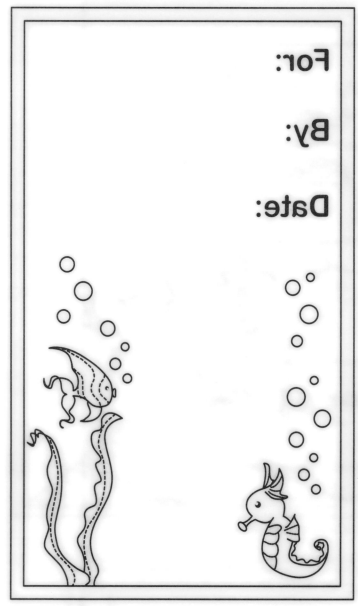

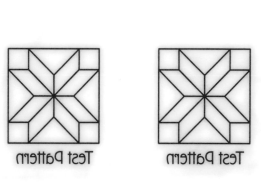

Use for Iron-On Transferring

Once Upon a Time...

To: _____

Stitched by: _____

Date: _____

Use for Iron-On Transferring

A Gift for You

Once Upon a Time...

To: _____

Stitched by: _____

Date: _____

A Gift for You

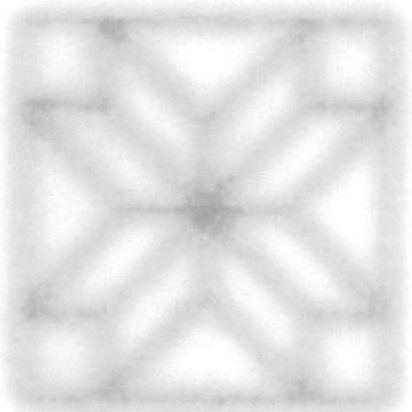

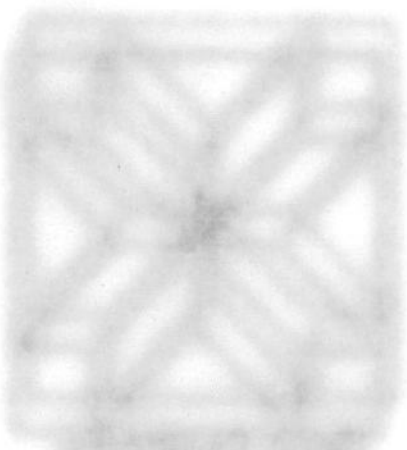

Made With Love for:

A Gift for You

Use for Iron-On Transferring

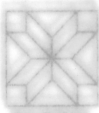

Made by:

For:

Date:

Made With Love for:

A Gift for You

Made by:

For:

Date:

Test Pattern

Test Pattern

Made With Love for:

Use for Iron-On Transferring

Made by:

For:

Date:

Made With Love for.

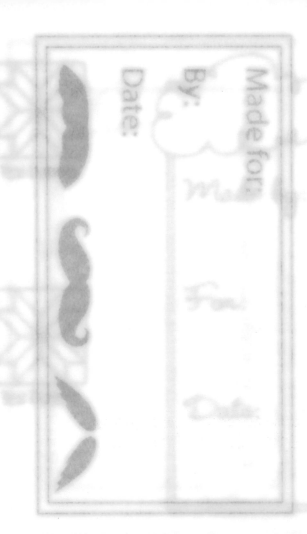

Made for:

By:

Date:

QUILTED BY:

DATE:

Quilted for a Favorite Teacher

QUILTED BY:

DATE:

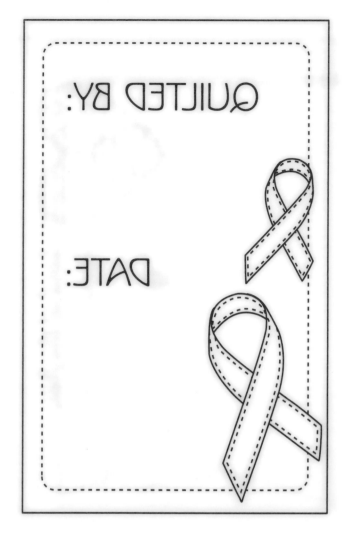

Made for:

By:

Date:

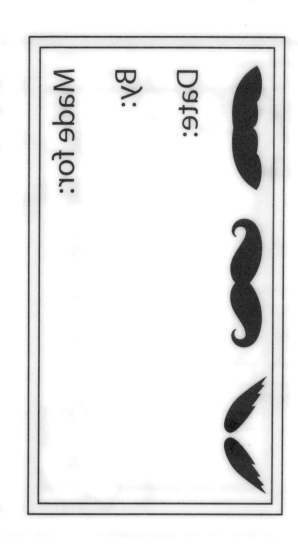

Quilted for a Favorite Teacher

Made for:

By:

Date:

QUILTED BY:

DATE:

Quilted for a Favorite Teacher

By

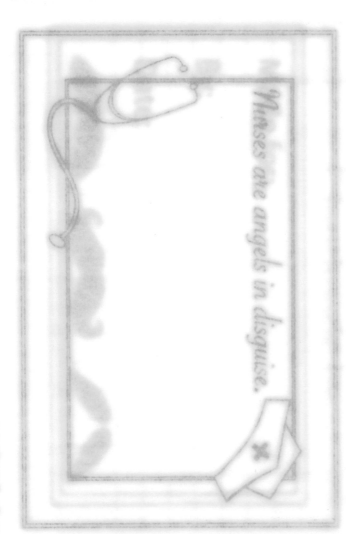

Nurses are angels in disguise.

QUILTED

land of the free,
home of the brave

DATE

Quilted for a favorite teacher

Quilted for:

By:

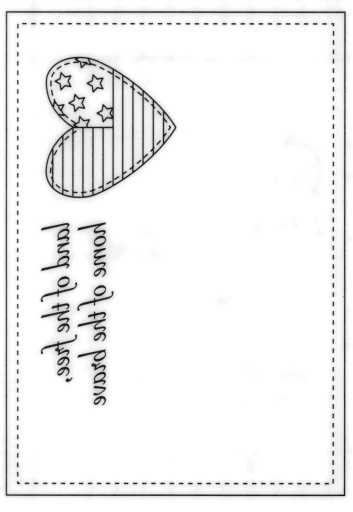

land of the free,
home of the brave

Nurses are angels in disguise.

Quilted for:

By:

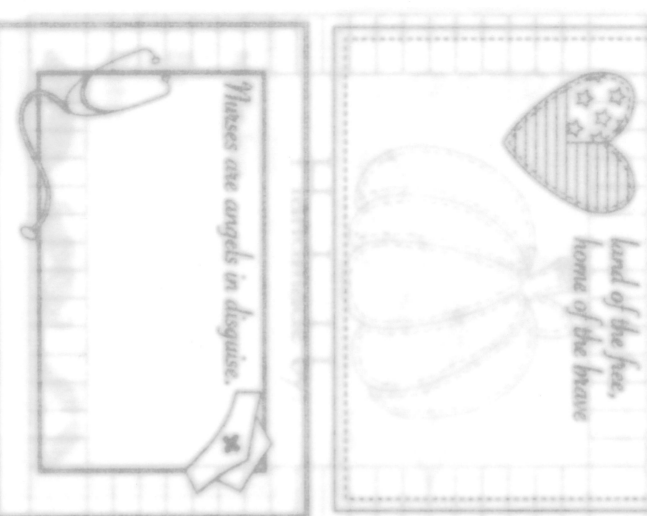

Nurses are angels in disguise.

land of the free, home of the brave

Quilted for:

Faith, Hope, Love

By:

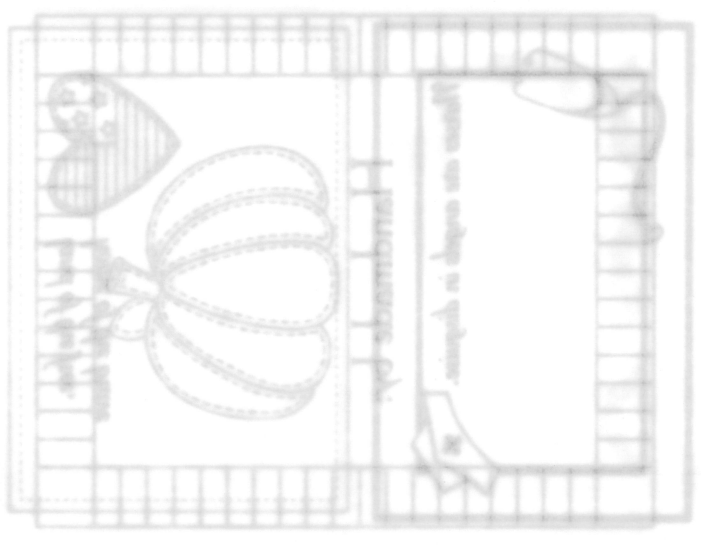

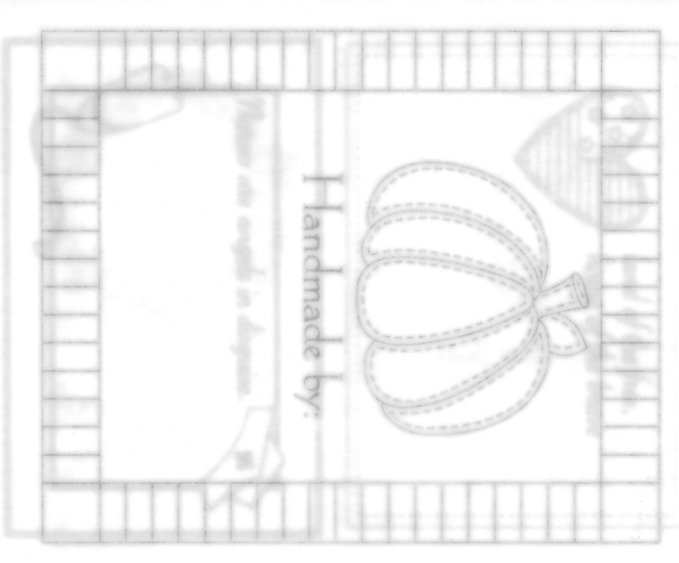

Handmade by:

Quilted for:

Faith, Hope, Love

By:

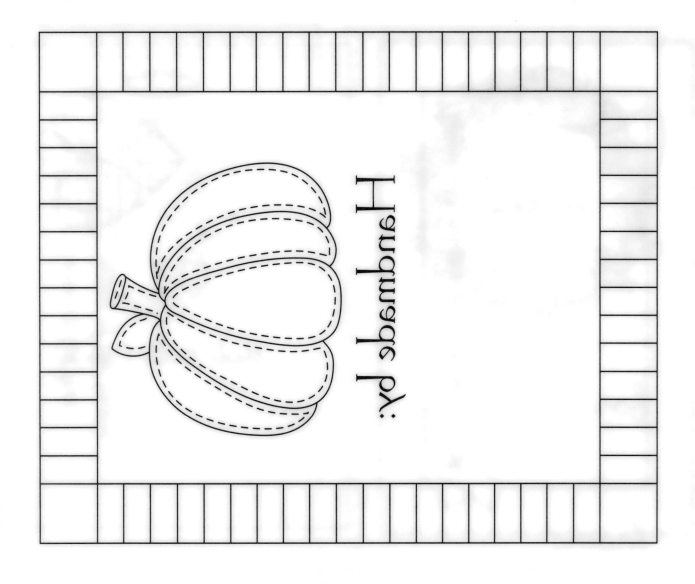

Handmade by:

Faith, Hope, Love

noel

Handmade by:

Faith, Hope, Love

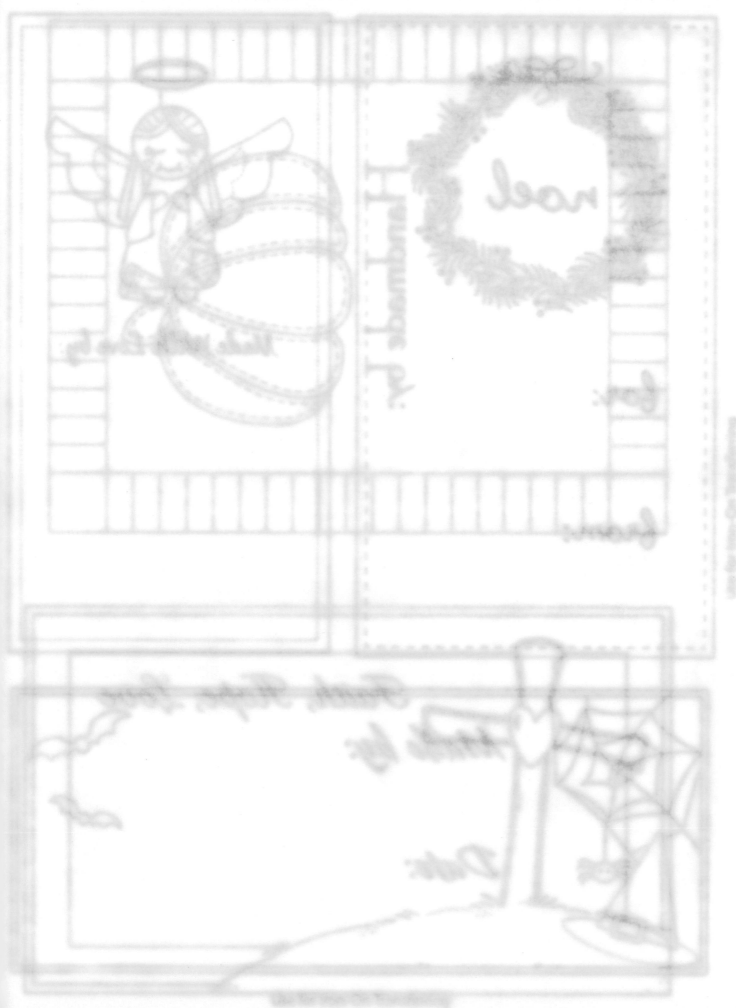

noel

for:

from:

Made With Love by:

Made by:

Date:

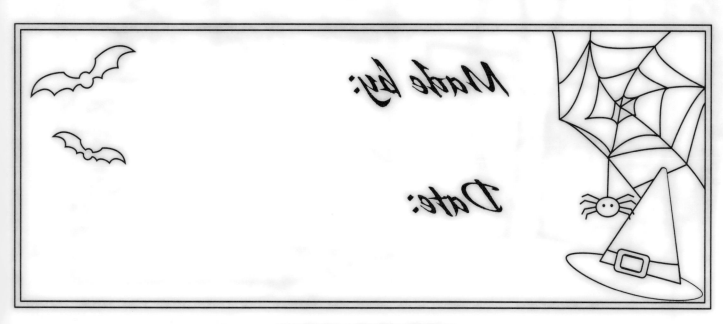

noel

for:

from:

Made With Love by:

Made by:

Date:

Merry Christmas!

noel

For:

From:

For Something Special

Merry & bright

Made by:
For:
Date:

For:
By:
Date:

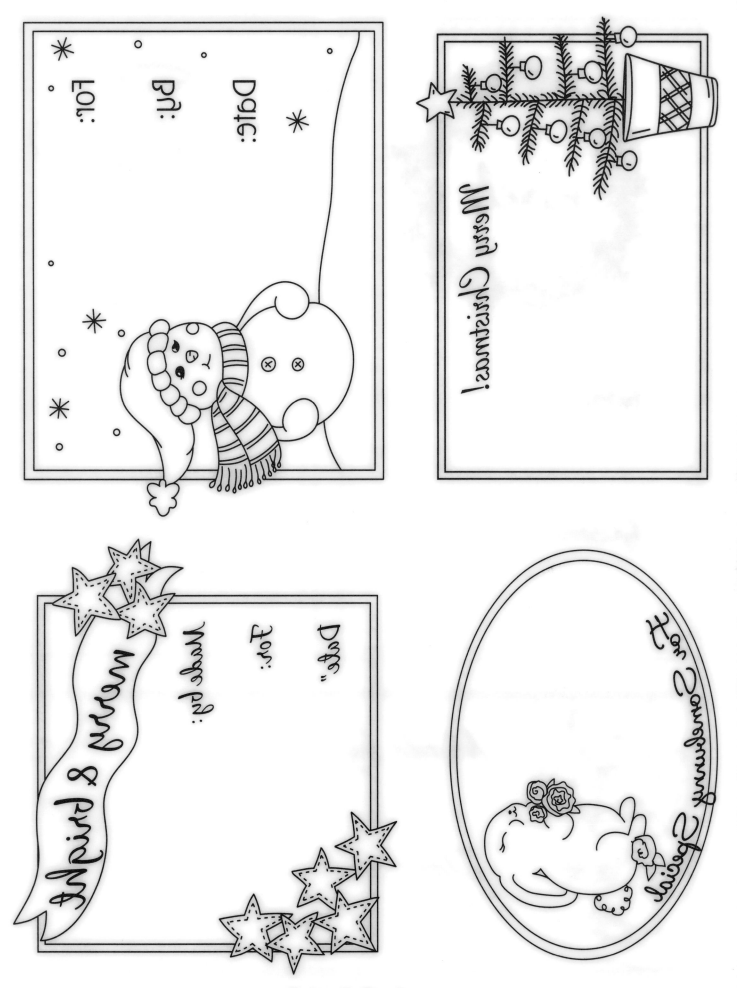

Date:

For:

From:

Merry Christmas!

Date:

For:

Made by:

Merry & Bright

Someone Special

Use for Iron-On Transferring

Merry Christmas!

For:
By:
Date:

For Somebunny Special

merry & bright
Made by:
For:
Date: